My Journey Through Divorce, Marriage, and Blended Family

Claudette T. Mullgrav Hutchinson

DEDICATION

I give thanks to Jesus Christ who never left me and never forsook me. Jesus Christ was with me during the darkest parts of my life and brought me out.

I dedicate this book to my wonderful children who have taught me a great deal about myself. They have allowed me to make mistakes, but never stopped supporting me, even when things seemed crazy.

Names have been changed to protect the privacy of individuals.

Such names are designated with an asterisk (*).

CONTENTS

Part One

Part Two

Part I

CHAPTER 1
"What Do I Do Next?"

Oh my God! I am divorced! The papers are signed. And people's lives have been moved around like chess pieces. I am leaving the court house thinking how easy this process was, but now the real work begins.

I am in my van moving through the streets, looking at all the different buildings, and realizing that I am behind the wheel – but how did I get here?! I now understand the lyrics of the song, "Your body's here with me, but your mind is on the other side of town."

Driving, I feel like I am having an "out of body" experience. I am shocked when I turn into the driveway of my apartment.   I didn't realize that I was home. *"Is this home?" "Where is home?"" What do I do next?"* My entire identity has been stolen from me. My innocence has been stolen. All that is left is a shell of who I used to be. It's insane to get up one morning as Mrs., and by the end of a business day, be half of a person as Ms. In a moment, after just signing some documents, feeling like this marriage never existed.

It seems like all of the breath has been ripped from my chest. My question is still, "What do I do next?"

I tried to go to a place in my mind, where it is peaceful and free, but it won't work. For a quick second, I forget who I am! Then a burst of reality sets in as the six little people whom God has given me charge over come running across the threshold of the front door to meet me as I enter. The children help me stay grounded in this physical world because they inspire me to not give up on living. They push me into living, trying, moving, learning, loving, and hoping for a better tomorrow.

All that day there was a question that kept swirling around in my head: "What should I do next?" I don't have the luxury of breaking down, or even falling apart, because of the six little lives that depend on me to push forward and live. I need to find the strength that God has given me to remember He will never leave me. I need to "muster up" all the faith that was deposited into me by my former Pastor and First Lady, the Embry's. They taught me to never give up and always continue to fight. This faith will help me get past the pain of such a great loss. The children didn't have a choice to be born into this life or this family. Now, their lives were being destroyed and ripped apart by the two adults they trusted the most - mother and father - in their lives.

My Journey Through Divorce, Marriage and Blended Family

What did I do next? As I am writing this chapter, I remember how easy it would have been to lose myself, but I came to a realization. It's nothing profound, it's just called "moving on!" My moving on meant starting dinner. I was thinking we could try something new and tasty, but the kids needed something normal, comfortable and steady. Stability was what my children needed, not me trying to be creative and fancy. My children's whole world had been turned upside down. Who was I to make any more changes in their lives?

CHAPTER 2
"The Process"

This is the way our new process began. The family which was once so happy together, full of love surrounding all of us, came crashing down like the towers on 9-11. It was daddy, mommy and the children all together at the same address, sharing the day-to-day happenings of life. There were some many good times just sitting around the table eating and drinking, never realizing how special those times were until they were over.

We shared many wonderful holidays such as Mother's Day, Father's Day, and birthdays. Then suddenly, we're sharing every other weekend. We (the parents) exchanged the children and pretended to put on a happy face for our little ones. We were faking like we were content with our broken lives. For the sake of the children, we tried to "play nice" and engaged in small talk while in their presence. We are just passing by one another, not sharing our dreams, hopes and goals anymore.

It was crazy. When I looked at my former husband, I used to see a beautiful picture of our future. But after it all came crashing down, I just see an empty canvas. It was as if the paint brush was lying lifeless on the table and the old paint cans had tumbled over.

I looked at him and he looked at me knowing that each one of us helped to destroy our wonderful family. I would love to believe one person was more responsible than the other for the breakup of this marriage, but I knew that wasn't true.

The two broken-hearted parents searched for answers for why it didn't work. I wondered what I could have done differently, contemplating where to place the blame. After beating myself up emotionally, I came to the conclusion that nothing would ever be the same. All I wanted was a place to retreat after such an ordeal known to me now as Divorce.

***

While I have finally gotten through the entry of the first battle, it's time to get on with our living. I needed to pick up the broken soldiers, which are my wounded children: Jaz'men, Janice, Jocelyn, Jacques, Jeremy, and Ja'eda. Those are the names that are recorded on their birth certificates, but mostly, engraved in my heart. For the sake of the children, I just had to gather my wounded heart, tuck it away and do the best I could.

My Journey Through Divorce, Marriage and Blended Family

This mess, which is called my life, now gives me something to work with and to work on. **Once you admit that you're broken inside, it's time to begin the healing process.** It's important to know that all of God's grace and mercy will help you through every minute, every hour, and every day. Just trust Him.

Life is work and you have to learn to be fearless and strong as declared in Psalm 139:14-15. Being fearless doesn't mean that you won't be afraid, or even wonder if you have made the right decisions. The journey from marriage through divorce can be adventurous or nightmarish. Once it begins, you must make a choice which is beneficial. During the process of Divorce (with the capital D), I faithfully asked God for directions every day. Then, I stood still and listened for His voice.

Don't move, unless God says so.

The thought I would love to convey to any parent going through Divorce is to learn to be obedient to God! Be authentic and get involved in mending your life. You must love God and learn to love yourself again. Believe that you deserve to be free.

Deliverance is a process. Once you get there, you must fight to stay grounded in that place. Just know that God cannot use you if you are unhealthy; you must be whole and present. "Believe God is able to do all things but fail!" (Ephesians 3:20) There is no failure in God. Just take one step forward and when you look down, you will realize that it is God that is carrying you.

CHAPTER 3
I Am Responsible For My Life

Once you have committed to a divorce, or a breakup of any kind, let the breakup be clear and clean in all aspects.

Just follow me through this next part.

I sat down one day and made a mental list of how we would separate the household items. The main thing you must remember is to be fair at all times! Always be true to who you serve and be a person after God's own heart. In many cases when a family is breaking up, **there is so much anger and hurt that the lines are blurred and it's hard to make fair and clear decisions.** I realized that it was hard because I allowed fear to creep in. Don't toss God aside. Remember, God should always be allowed to lead and guide us in every decision. I couldn't pick and choose when I wanted to be led and when I wanted to follow; I had to completely trust Him.

Once I came to that conclusion, I came to this: I am responsible for my own life. I am willing to take responsibility for me, and no one else.

With that realization, the mental list began to form. Each item given up or taken away, I remembered that children were involved in the splitting of the family. The thought that stood out in my mind was that my children needed to have two comfortable homes to live in. (You do not want to be the parent who causes your children any more pain then they're going through when losing the stability of a two-parent home.) Keeping a table or chair doesn't really mean that much to you… but it was the parting with the things that made it all so real.

When I was overtaken with such great emotions of loss, I couldn't see clearly. The hurt ran over me like a river in the middle of a perfect storm. While you are in the eye of the storm isn't the best time to make decisions. Be cautious in your decision-making; proceed slowly. It's difficult to toss around the idea of a new life when you have not yet released the old one. My thoughts were always on what God would think of me.

"There hath no temptation taken you, but such as is common to man; but God is faithful, who will not suffer you to be tempted above that ye are able; but will with the temptation also make a way to escape, that ye may be able to bear it." (1 Corinthians 10:13)

The true purpose of the word of God for me at that point was comfort. When you are going through your "valley lows", Jesus Christ will come and give you hope. When darkness comes, the word will shine a light on it. How I handled challenging situations in my darkest time defined my character. I was able to find joy while fighting through the smoke screen of my crazy life, and I came through victoriously. I had some battle scares, but I never gave up.

Let's wrap it up.

When making your mental list, split everything evenly. When the day came to execute the split, I was right where you are now. I kept looking at my children. I embraced and encouraged them to spend a lot time with their father. I didn't want them to feel uncomfortable and unhappy. I said to myself often, "So Claudette, don't be selfish when the children want to be with their dad." I love my children enough to want them to have a solid relationship with him and it didn't undermine their relationship with me.

When I took responsibility for my life, I stopped holding on to things that were insignificant. I realized God wanted me to have great peace, love, and joy, even when I was going through the heat of the fight with my ex-husband. For me, releasing everything to God was the most liberating experience in my journey after my divorce. Once I had that freedom, nothing could hold me back.

Don't allow the devil to release pain, fear, misunderstanding, and doubt on you. "Believe that God is able to do all things." (Ephesians 3:20).

CHAPTER 4
I Began to Question God

Even after I accepted responsibility of my life, there was still healing work that needed to be done. At this point, I began to question God.

Why me, God?

What will I do now, God?

Where will I go from here, God?

There were so many changes happening at once. I quickly forgot all that I had learned in the years that I had been with the Lord. Many times during the divorce, I felt like I had come out of a physical fight, not a spiritual one. The scripture always makes it clear for me:

"For we wrestle not against flesh and blood, but against principalities, against powers, against the rulers of the darkness of this world, against spiritual wickedness in high places". (Ephesians 6:12)

Sometimes my flesh wanted some satisfaction. So I daydreamed of slapping my former husband. I truly believed that he had destroyed our lives and our happy home. The carnal man was trying to take over and I had to stop listening to the devil!!!!!

I turned my face to the wall, like Hezekiah did when the Prophet told him that he was going to die (Isaiah 38:2). Turn to the Prince of Peace when things are tough. There were times I didn't believe that God was listening to me. There were times I felt like God had forsaken me. My faith seemed to be draining right out of my body. It was as if I could not catch my breath. I was so angry with God because the relationship did not last! The house had crumbled and the end was near. What shall I do now?

It was in these times when the spirit of God, the Holy Ghost, surfaced and rose up in me like a mighty warrior. I was just crazy enough to believe that God took time to create me and He wouldn't leave me. I was doing all the right things: serving, worshipping, paying tithes, and loving God's people. Feeding the hungry and getting the Gospel out was my life. It was astonishing that it was my marriage that was erased.

The worst thing that arose in my spirit was that my **trust** and my **faith** were wavering. On the inside, I was screaming and trembling, but on the outside, I looked okay. The natural man in me would say things to make me question God's holy will like, "There are child molesters, killers, and people who live just to make life hard for others and I am being punished. But this is happening to *me*, your *servant*." In my mind, these people - the child molesters, killers, and rapists were worthy of death. Not me.

But God, in His wisdom, saw me sitting in the middle of the floor, without the physical strength to get up. At this point, God allowed His mercy, His love, and His peace to overtake me. Acts 2:2 declares,

"And suddenly there came a sound from heaven as of a rushing mighty wind, and it filled the house where they were sitting."

While I was sitting on that floor crying and weeping, God helped me to see that He is God and there is none other. The devil is depending on me to be sitting in the dark and crying because I was broken, angry, disturbed, and hurt. But God! My strength began to take hold and the Holy Spirit brought the Word back to my remembrance. The voice of the Lord spoke to me and said, *"For the Lord thy God is a merciful God. He will not forsake thee, neither destroy thee, nor forget the covenant of thy fathers which he swore unto them."* (Deuteronomy 4:31)

It took months for me to allow God's voice to rein in me every day. Once I came back to my true self, I began to speak the Word daily. The moment I gave myself completely to God and accepted the hand that was dealt to me, it seemed as though the foul ground was broken up and the Almighty had something to work with. My confidence was built up, and I knew the storm would be conquered. My mind, my heart, and my spirit caught up with each other. At that moment, I got off of the floor and took a soothing bath to clear my mind. Sometimes you must give yourself time to grieve and breathe.

I knew my next step. Life began and I was never the same again. The most important thing I received from this challenge in my life was the knowledge "that there was nothing too hard for my God" (Genesis 18:9-15).

There is one condition: continue to serve Him, regardless of what transpired. Believe in GOD!

CHAPTER 5
Letting Go

I wish you love. I wish you shelter from the storm. I wish you warmth from the open fire. I wish you hope for tomorrow. I wish that all your dreams come true. I wish you great joy. I wish you much peace. I wish you happiness and never loneliness. I wish you freedom. I wish you truth and understanding. But most of all, my love, I wish you love that words can't describe. I never thought that I would be saying GOODBYE, my love.

There is a great deal of love missing when a relationship falls apart and a family is smashed into pieces. Sometimes one party wants to move on and the other party is standing still, unwilling to release the past.

I was contemplating walking through that door called My Future. I believed that marriage and love should last forever. The love that God demonstrates is forever. The love that man creates in his imagination elevates a great expectation which most people cannot aspire to reach.

I watch love stories on television that say that love

conquers all. That is not always the way it goes in real life. I am not saying that a person cannot attain an endless love. But an endless love, the kind you see on television, takes two people working every single day on the total functions of communication, respect, understanding, and trust. Other aspects, including the financial support, rearing of the children, and a spiritual relationship with God, must be mastered.

There are a great many things that should be discussed before two people say, "I do."

Letting go is tough, but you can do it. Just don't live in what was. LET THE PAST GO. I realized that if I didn't, I would never reach the level of love I desired for my life. I couldn't make my former husband love me. There is an old saying that if a person really belongs with you, let them go. If they come back, they belong to you for all the time.

The reason you want to believe this saying is true because having faith is very important to us. How do you really let it all go? It's like opening your hand and letting something fall out. It's that easy just try. Relationships are hard to keep together, but breaking up was much worse. I really needed God's help.

We have come to the end of our journey. Some battles were won and some were lost. But most of all, the little soldiers have come through the war. The battle scars are healed and new skin has surfaced. I have loved, lost, and tears have been wiped away. Forgiveness has been found.

The lesson I have learned throughout the divorce process, is that God hates divorce. But I am saying to God I am here, where is here **divorced**.

God, what shall I do? I have allowed my flesh to be in charge. I have listened to my feelings, and now I need to hear from you.

Where are you, Master?

Please don't forsake me while I am in this pit.

I continued to pray, fast, and seek God. I didn't have the luxury of completely falling apart because my children needed me, and I needed God.

I must answer your unanswered question: how do I know God hates divorce?

He created the family - both husband and wife (Genesis 2:7; Genesis 2:22). He created family before the church (Matthew 16:18): *I will build my church.* The scripture tells us that they become one flesh. I know that we must trust the scripture and believe it is true. I truly believe God hates divorce because family are ripe apart, houses are separated, children are committing suicide and there are a host of other issues arising from divorced families. I am not saying divorce destroys every family but at least 50 percent.

God was not silent during the darkest part of my life

and he won't be silent in yours. Please trust me!

PART II

CHAPTER 1
Who's in Your Life Now?

"I married my husband and he made me feel safe. I could look in his eyes and see myself. Then, one day, I took a mental snapshot of my life, and I wasn't there. There were moments when I could see my shadow leaving my body. I began to reach for hope and hope floated away from me. Faith was just beyond my grasp. And when my mind leaped for it, it slipped right between the cracks. Just one look and I was gone. Then some good days arrived and my smile reappeared. Life started having meaning because I tried to give love and Love came right back to me.

You never know, just one look might bring love and life. JUST ONE LOOK. JUST ONE LOOK."

Wow! I didn't really know what to do. I felt that I was past all those old feelings from my past relationship. It had been a year since the divorce, and I was exploring the desire to meet someone new. My first thought was that the children had only seen me with their father. How would they feel to see me with another man other than their dad? There are so many questions flying through my head.

I had children at home. What would people think? Would my family accept someone new? Would he be a good match for my life? I was a mom who was not trying to bring a lot of men in front of my children. Did I have time to date? How could I date and start a new business? Well, this is how it happened.

The man who came into my life was a gentleman from my past. Pop. I had known Pop since I was 15 years old. I was just head-over-heels in love with him when I was a teenager. The only problem was he was dating my best friend Sophia. In my generation, we didn't steal or sleep around with our friend's boyfriend.

Sophia never knew how I much I cared for him. It seemed like fate; Sophia practically put us together. She was cheating on Pop with another friend of ours, so it was my job to keep him busy while she was with the other guy. During that time, I got to know Pop and his family. I began to care for him deeply. Pop never knew at that time I loved him. It was so easy to love Pop. There were many things happening in his life at that point, so he decided that he did not want to complicate my life any further. So, he made the choice to walk out of my life without any notice. I did not go looking for him at that point in my life because I was used to people walking out on me. My home life was crazy; I chalked it up to the fact that I wasn't good enough and life rolled on. I realized that we all have to choose what is best for us.

My Journey Through Divorce, Marriage and Blended Family

Now, twenty years later, Pop appeared at my grandmother's house, in Atlanta, Georgia. He wanted to know how he could contact me. He left his business a card with my grandmother. My grandmother contact him and gave him the phone number of my church. After speaking with my grandmother, Pop had a conversation with his young brother. During their conversion, his baby brother informed him that I "was the one that he should have married". He told him that he had seen me at South DeKalb Mall a few months ago, and that I was a church girl, and that I had five or six kids.

One Sabbath (Saturday) afternoon, Pop decided to call me at the church. One of the Deacons informed me that I had a phone call and to pick up in the office. He greeted me by my nickname, but I didn't recognize his voice.

He started the conversation by talking about a Diana Ross concert I wanted to attend when I was 16 years old. No one knew about that except Pop; I finally recognized his voice. And at that moment I started screaming! I was over-joyed to hear his voice after twenty-four years.

CHAPTER 2
Yes, Mom's Dating

After that day Pop and I began to get reacquainted, sometime had passed. Then he finally asked me out on a date. It was scary, and exciting but I went out with him anyway.

On our dinner date, I laughed and enjoyed sitting across the table from him. Our date lasted over four hours. Before we knew it, we looked around the restaurant and most of the people in there were gone. When the date came to an end Pop dropped me off at my mother's home. I could feel he wanted to kiss me, and I wanted to kiss him but I wasn't ready. He was a gentleman.

The next morning when the family began moving about the house, I didn't say much that morning trying to avoid conversion. But the children started asking me about my whereabouts on last evening. Because they were not accustomed to me being out late on a Saturday night. I didn't feel very comfortable giving them any answer, so I lied. I deflected and turn the focus from me back to them the best way I knew how. I'm the mom, but I was as scared as a little girl back in a corner that morning. After that first date, I spent a lot of time hiding my whereabouts when the relationship was new and fresh. I wasn't ready to bring a man in front of my children. So, when the children were spending time with their dad, Pop and I spent a lot of time together. As we became more acquainted with each other, we talked every night. Things seemed awkward at first because we had both enjoyed being married, and now we were divorced, and now we are dating. This was strange to me I don't know if it was strange to him. The most difficult part for me was the physical contact it was nice, but we had to always stop at a certain point because we were not married he was not **my husband.** So we couldn't share those intimate moments, but there was a kind of love he shared with me that physical touch could not reach. He could touch me without his hands, he could reach me without words. This man gave me the kind of intimacy that made sex just surface stuff. I never knew a love like this. He reach a part of my heart I never knew existed.

As our relationship progressed, we decided to involve our children. The older children – his and mines - had a difficult time at first. However, as time passed, we continued to communicate and showed them that we loved them. As time passed things got easier. The wonderful thing about our children is they like each other and the learned from each other.

Children adjust a lot better if you're honest with them. I didn't start off being honest, thinking I was protecting them and it back-fired. The children wanted to be a part from the very start of the relationship. Adult must choice what works best for their situation. After all, we wanted to do what was best for all the children. The children needed and deserved a healthy and safe place to run too. I wanted us to be that safe place.

What about you?

Dating turned into to marriage, and a blended family. Then I had some new question that only God could answer. How is this new family going to work? I kept thinking and wanting my life to smooth out. But here I go again, jumping into my mess, which is called my life. I am never afraid to jump in and do the work. So, I am saying to my audience please get involved. Don't be afraid that it might hurt. But in the end, we are called FAMILY. We end up having a wonderful blended family. God really showed us how to maneuver through this new family and everybody lived. Was it difficult at time yes but was it worth it YES! Step parenting is not for the faint of heart. I truly believe that being a step-parent was a gift to me from God. I was given a charge and I fumble at times but more than enough as mommy I won the race. This is just a little side bar for people who are thinking about dating someone with children (male or female) you, should not take this task lightly, because you can change the course of a young person life for the good or bad.

Which one will **you** choose good or bad?

CHAPTER 3
Loyalty to the Biological Parent

Families remind me of ants: when they work together, they build a fortress. Families are the same: families build fortified relationships, even when we are different. The relationship is unconditional. Family is building relationships, one block at a time. Even if it fails, you begin again and never give up on them when you're unhappy.

Mom and Dad begin the journey for the family, but the children round everything off, and complete the circle of life - for our family. Family create their heritage and memories, which last throughout all eternity. Families don't always get it right, but fight to have dream. When members of the family don't get it right, the family continues to move forward.

I come from a dysfunctional family, but it's still family. Know that no family is the same and we all have to develop. Family doesn't always mean same blood running through your veins. Who defines your Family? God said in the scripture, "who is my mother and who is my family?" (Matthew 12:48).

Families dream together, and when dreams are far from reach, the family is still there. Just when you believe you can't make it, family brings you back from that deep mountain which is too hard to climb. Family is as family does: one unit, bound together and unbroken. When a link in the chain is broken, like a divorce or death of a child, we band together and cover one another in love and peace.

 Who wants a family?

WHAT IS FAMILY TO YOU?

When you are married, especially if there is a blended family, there are so many challenges. It is evident that there are going to be struggles for power and respect. Just imagine the woes of the relationship when families have to merge.

The children in a divorced home really do not get a voice in the matter. The adults are making every decision. Where will they live? What will they will eat, how will visitation be handled, and who gets what weekends? Each adult in this messy drama should just stop, take a breath, and start listening. These small steps will save you some heartaches.

I strongly felt that the main challenge in a blended family is learning to respect the rules of the natural parent's household without giving up the bounty in your home. Each adult must take a stand and have heart and strength to know what's best for the children. Secondly, the natural, or biological parent, and new spouse should not ever allow the children to cause conflict within their marital relationship. Children are smarter than we give them credit for. They know how to play parents against each other. The Bible reminds us that the father and mother must cleave to one another. The adults must show good leadership even though mistakes are made.

Another difficultly I ran into was when I fell in love with my step-children and their biological family members felt as though I was stealing them away from their mother, because the children called me mom. I never asked my step daughters to call me mom. I just treated them like I birthed them into the world. Loving all four of them was easy. But at times, the children felt like they were betraying their mother because they cared for me. I was very up front with their biological mother; I had an honest talk with her and a good line of communication opened up. It doesn't always happen that way.

The children seemed to struggle with whether they could accept the love that I had to offer. As a step-parent, I believe it is important to keep a level head and be patient. I couldn't always speak when I was angry or hurt. I sometimes felt like an outsider with my step children, as well with my biological children. It's tough when you are always trying to be the good guy and things would still be wrong. There were times I just wanted to scream. Then I remembered the word of God and it reminded me to "forgive seven times seventy". (Matthew 18:22) That wasn't always easy but it can be done. My step-children had lost their family as well. So, now we are blending some more wounded soldiers.

I have endured a great deal of emotional challenges

during this journey of bringing two families together without starting a war. We must allow the Holy Ghost to lead and guide us the rest of the way when we are weary. All of my Christian life I have read that we must "acknowledge Him and He will direct our paths" (Proverbs 3:6). As a step-parent, I offended God a great many times by trying to help Him out. But I realized quickly that He didn't need my assistance!

This is a BIG one when it's time to discipline the children. Each biological parent should handle the discipline until the family adjusts to the new family unit. Next, try to refrain from using the term "step". The step-parent may feel a little left out, but in the long run, this will keep down a great deal of confusion. In my blended family, my husband and I set the ground work for how we would run our home. You have to do what works for your family. When my husband and I got married, we blended ten children together. I know I said to refrain from you using the term "step". But for the purpose of writing this chapter, I use this term so you will know who's who. One of my step-daughters was very protective of her biological mother. When I would make the simplest comment about hair or clothing, sparks would ignite. She perceived my words as disrespect to her mother. I would just simply express to her to try something new or different. But it is my job, no matter how hard, to ask God to teach me how to relate to her to show her that I loved her. If I lead, she would follow, just as I followed God, the Master.

My Journey Through Divorce, Marriage and Blended Family

There were times when the children felt a little uncomfortable in our new blended family. We would have family meetings, special outings, trips, dinners, and family nights. When planning events, my husband and I made sure that we included each and every child - regardless of where they lived by calling ahead of time so everyone was involved. This fosters love and respect among the children. The children saw us working at being a tight unit. Love is not what is said, but what is demonstrated.

It was easy to love my stepdaughters. However, I never made the mistake of telling them that I was their friend. It is difficult to come through unchartered waters, but I used Jesus as my guide. I made a lot of mistakes, but I always loved all the children. I really believe they loved and respected (and still do love and respect) me as well. Gaining their respect was important to me.

I talked to all the children as this book was developing in my heart. We have ten children together and most of them are happy, healthy, and emotionally sound. When they are hurting, sometimes I cry when I'm listening to their life stories. I cry because I feel my choices are the reason they are hurting. There are times when we take a step back into the past. All of us want to be free, but we don't always stay that way. But I am striving to stay free. One way to stay free is to not make decisions according to hurt anymore and during times when I am in distress.

As we grow and develop, I have learned that God is

merciful and kind.   At times it was difficult for me as a parent to take responsibility for how my actions and the negative affect it had on the children. Parents don't always feel like they should say, "I am sorry." Please let me give you some advice: Say it. "I am sorry." Saying sorry means your behavior will change. Did you just have an 'Aha' moment?

CHAPTER 4
The Voices

Part A. Voices of Adult Children of Divorce

*Alonzo's Story

Alonzo is a very intelligent young man. I have known him since he was a baby. His parent's break-up was a very public divorce, but he hasn't allowed anything to stop him from becoming successful.

1. *How old were you when your parents divorced?*
   - I was eleven years old.

2. *After going through the divorce, at such a young age what are your feelings on divorce now?*

   - My thoughts on divorce haven't changed as I have gotten older. In some marriages, divorce is inevitable. People change and outgrow each other. I do know that it takes two people to fight for their relationship. I know marriage takes work.

3. *Will you ever get married?*

- Yes, definitely. It makes me cherish the relationship I have with others now. My parents' divorce has caused me to be more accepting of peoples' short comings.

4. *Did your parents handle you and your brother in a caring way during the divorce process?*

- Yes, but it did bring up some questions in my mind. It has caused me to be cautious when choosing my girlfriends. I won't rush into marriage. As I think about it now, I really did turn to my parents for help with the divorce. I turned to my coaches and my close friends. But to be honest, I kept a lot inside.

5. *How is your relationship with your father?*

- During that time, I really distanced myself from him. I turned to my coaches to guide me through troubling situations. Now that I am a man, Dad and I are good. During the divorce, my way of dealing with stuff, was to push my parents away.

6. *How is your relationship with your mother?*

- During the divorce, my grandparents and friends helped me emotionally. Mom and I had a bumpy road at times, but we are good now.

7. Did you have issues trusting women because of the divorce?

- Yes, but I started hanging around my grandmother and the trust and love for women grew.

8. How do you see women now that you are a man, and a child of divorce?

- I really connect well with women, because I was raised by a single mom. But the one thing I try to do is to be real with them.

Joni's* Story

Joni is the oldest, biological daughter of a clan close to me.

1. *How do you feel about your dad being married to your stepmother?*

   - I feel like they make a great team.

2. *Do you and your stepmother communicate?*

   - Yes, we communicate very well.

3. *Does she love you and your children?*
   - I can honestly say, "Yes, she does love us."

4. *Does your stepmother accept you for who you are?*

   - She has always accepted me for who I am. No matter what I believe, she will always.

5. *Does your stepmother try to keep lines of communication open when there are disagreements between you and your father?*

   - Yes! She has always been that third party who can get my father to see both sides of the issues. She knows how to speak to his heart.

6. *How does it feel having so many siblings from your new family?*

   - At first I felt hurt. I felt that they were getting everything that I wanted from my father. But after a lot of praying and getting to know my brothers and sisters, I was happy and excited. I even started to feel special. Now, at this moment in my life, I thank God for them, and my kids have aunts and uncles that love them. I am very blessed.

7. *When you found out that your dad was married again, what was your first reaction?*

   - Goodness! When I heard I was like "Oh no, not again!" I just prayed that she was the one.

8. *Are you and your stepmother close?*

   - I wouldn't say close, due to me being very private and keeping things to myself. But, we have our own type of bond. I do believe, if I was more open, then we would be closer.

9. *Is she a good grandmother to your children?*

   - She's a great grandmother to my kids. She loves them, unconditionally.

10. *Do you trust your stepmother with your heart?*

- It's hard for me to trust, period. So I can say I do somewhat trust her, but that's how I feel about anyone. But mama puts her heart out there.

11. *Did you feel disloyal to your biological mother by caring for your stepmother?*

- No, I never felt disloyal to my mother. I have been through so much with my biological mother in the past. I was happy to have my stepmother in my life. She kind of made up for the lack of motherly guidance I was missing.

My Journey Through Divorce, Marriage and Blended Family

Gabriella's* Story

Gabriella is the second-oldest, biological daughter of her blended clan. She is the child who is the most raw and honest. One day, she said to her mother during Passover, "Mom, you lied to me. You said everything was going to be alright, but it's not." This was just a few weeks before her mother told all the children that they wouldn't be getting back together.

1. *When did you realize your parents weren't going to stay together?*

   - At first, I thought it was the day we left. I was about 12 years old and my parents had just had a fight, a really big fight. Afterwards, my mom came in our room and told us to pack a bag. It was the middle of the afternoon when we arrived at my grandmother's house. We stayed about two or three days before anyone made any reference to going home. But what I noticed most was my mother's demeanor. It was so different, in what I now know as a good different. She was so much calmer, like being away from my dad gave her some kind of inner peace. This is the day I thought I realized it. But one day, my mother looked into my oldest sister's eyes as she asked why did mom let this happen to us. At that moment, something in my mom's eyes went dark, and I knew my parents' marriage had lost its life.

2. *How old were you when they separated?*

- I was 12 years old, a few months shy of my 13th birthday. I call this my see-and-decide point in my life. I was old enough to see things for what they really were. I was also old enough to decide what I saw was for me or not.

3. Please give me your true feelings on divorce?

- From the kid in me, divorce sucks major apples. But I am sure my mother, your author, would like me to be a little more descriptive. So, here it goes. Divorce is something I never wanted to experience as a child and even more as a wife. Divorce is the only thing that ever made me feel like I was broken. My family has gone through highs, lows, and middles. But my parents' divorce was what I considered as six feet below. Just because divorce is common in the world, that does not make it acceptable in my world.

4. *By your parents divorcing, does that change your outlook on relationships?*

- Yes, it has. Like I said, I am a see-and–decide kind of person. So, it`s only logical that it would shape my own outlook on relationships. I learned that just because you love someone, doesn't mean you can make it through life with that someone. To be truly honest, it has made me very guarded as a woman. I say woman and not person because it's something about a broken heart that can really make a girl find a castle and stay there, protected and safe.

5. *Will you ever get married?*

- Will I or won't I? That's a good question. All I can say is that I don't see it, especially in my near future, but if it's God's plan... We shall see. But to be honest, divorce or no divorce, marriage has always been questionable for me. I don't know, I'm weird about a long-term commitment.

6. *Did your parents handle you and your siblings in a caring way during the period of pain when your family was breaking up?*

- The only way I could explain my parents' actions during the break up is to say that they tried. They did the best they knew how. So as an adult, I can see that they were just as lost in the situation as we were. But I like to know what is happening and how things will end. So them trying to protect us to the point that we didn't do enough talking about it. Actually, it meant just that it is how it will be from now on. One thing I know, my younger siblings felt like why are they doing this to me, to us? It's a hard question to answer as a big sister. It was rough, but we survived. I honor the two people who brought us into the world. God has balanced out my life in a way I didn't realize until writing this. In the end, I am blessed that they are a part of my life; I got dads!

7. *How is your relationship with your father since the divorce?*

- Stepdad, real dad, birth father, biological father, these are terms that no longer exist in my vocabulary. There's my dad and my bonus dad. We'll start with the first one. Kevin Johnson is now a senior. I feel the need to remind him how old he is getting, a family insider joke. It's like this. He was the first image of a man I ever saw, physically and spiritually. He is, and always will be, the first man I have ever loved. He is something to study for me because our facial features are not the only similarities. Our relationship has always been there for me to make sure he doesn't miss out on anything having to do with my siblings. Although we have not always used it, we've always had a line of communication. No matter how rough it gets, Kevin Johnson, Sr. will always be my funny, my love, my tears, my first, and one half of my

foundation. Now, bonus dad, Pop. This guy is so
opposite of me. It was a lot in the beginning.
He's a hugger, a smile, a good morning person,
and a million other things. I was not a fan in the
beginning. Everyone knows that I don't do new
people well. But he was persistent; he never let
me see him as a punk. Even when I was a brat,
he stuck in there. I will eternally be grateful for
him. He is still different from me, but now I
know we work, and that says a lot there. I trust in
those I feel trust worthy.

8. *How is your relationship with mom since the divorce?*

- Claudia, she's my mom and I love her. That's
not what she wants me to say, but I needed to
get that out, first. My mother and I have always
been close, and me being a very sick child, spent
more time with her than my other siblings
sometimes. She's my rock, my example, my
mother. Though the divorce, it was hard on me.
I would never, ever think less of her as a
woman. The fact that she has made it right with
God shows me not to hide away, but to go to
God, for myself. That is one of the most
important things she has ever taught me. Now,
as an adult, it's hard to put our relationship into
words without writing my own book. So I'll just
say we talk, we discuss, we debate, we pray, we
laugh and we love. It's ever changing.

9. Do you have an issue trusting men?

- I trust a person by their actions and intentions.
The gender of a person doesn't throw me off.
My family was broken, but not my trust in there
being good men in the world. If I'm honest, I
have always had more guy friends than women.
So that isn't a factor to me.

10. Is it hard for you to connect with men? If so, is it because of being from a divorced home?

- No. Men have never really been a problem for
me. Divorce happens to my whole family; it
involved my whole family, male and female. As
long as I have other connections, it will never be
a problem for me.

My Journey Through Divorce, Marriage and Blended Family

<u>Phillip's* Story</u>

During my vacation in New York City, this past year 2013, I was able to spend some time with my friend Phillip. We sat up until 4:00 a.m. talking. While we were talking and enjoying each other's company, we started talking about our childhood. I asked him if I could interview him for my book and he said yes. I was so excited, I immediately got pen and paper out and started digging through his life. He allowed me to ask any question and he was very frank with me.

He expressed to me how difficult it was during his childhood because his mom dated quite a bit when he was younger. "I want to make it very clear that she wasn't a promiscuous young lady. But because she dated a lot and lived with a few of her boyfriends, there wasn't a sense of closeness and community when you move a lot."

"During my junior year of high school, my mom realized that we needed a place we could call home. My mom never apologized for the way we lived or how it made me feel. I just had to move on and grow up and be my own man. Secondly, I needed to make sure that, if I have any children, they never, ever felt that way. I respect about my mom's conscious decision to change her life and behavior, she did it."

"My mother only had two children by two different

gentlemen. My biological father was never really a part of my life until I became a man. On my biological father's side, I have eight brothers and two sisters. But I have always lived around my little brother by my mom. Now, my mom is married to my stepfather. We have added to the family because he has two adult children. So, if you put us all together, it's twelve of us."

As I interviewed Phillip, he seemed to be very healthy emotionally. But as the interview went on, the strings began to unravel. As we talked, I could see the disconnect between him and his family. Phillip has never lived in the house while his biological parents were together. And as his mother is married now, he hasn't had the privilege to see his mom happily married while he resided in the same home with them. "When my mother married my stepfather, I was living with my grandmother before I attended my first year of college."

There was something special about Phillip and his mom's relationship. She was only seventeen years old when she got pregnant, so they grew up together. Phillip stressed to me that he was only introduced to his mom's serious relationships. She didn't have men in and out of the house when he was a child.

Phillip father and mother were only together about two years, but his brother, Daniel', father lived with them in the home for about eight years. His mom was in control of what was going on in the household. Some single parents leave their children to fend for themselves, but that was not the case in this household.

In 1999, Phillip mom purchased a house which provided them with a stable address. "By 2000, my mom met my step-father and they were married in 2004. There was a different air about our family because my stepfather was not Christian and my mom and brother are Christians. I am Catholic. It was a challenge to meet on common ground on a lot of issues."

During the interview, I got a funny feeling when I started asking him questions about his relationship with his stepfather. Phillip responded with one-word answers. So not to offend him, I rephrased my questions, still probing enough to get a good interview. I asked him very direct questions:

Did you feel like he was a good match for your mom?

"Yes, I think that they met each other's needs. But, I have never lived with them, as a couple, to really say any differently. I don't live my life by what people say or think. Who am I to judge the relationship?"

Do you have a favorite memory of yours as a family?

"When they got married, my brother and I gave her away at the wedding."

We began to speak on his personal feelings about marriage. My direct question to him was *"Is divorce an option when it comes to marriage?"*

"No. I feel like all situations can be worked through, if both people are willing to work together and they don't give up. As long as she doesn't cheat on me, I can handle just about anything else."

He said that he could work through anything, but he was talking about his former relationship and he seemed very harsh and he had written her off. I am not saying she hadn't done anything wrong, he just didn't seem to have any feeling for her anymore. I understood his reason because of the things he has been through. He wasn't going to put up with mess.

I was very curious about how they interacted as a family.

I asked him, *"How often do you guys hang out or have dinner as a family?"*

He said, "We have never been out as a family and I rarely go home to visit."

He had his reasons for why they couldn't spend time together. His main reason was because he moved closer to his job in Buffalo New York, which was an hour away. Then he said to me: "Girl, if you were not in town, I wouldn't have been here today." I asked why. He replied, "I am my own person."

What do you mean when you say that you are your own person?

"For example, when I go out of town, I don't have to tell anyone and I might be gone a few weeks."

I said, *If you go out of town, don't you call your mom, grandmother, or brother to let them know?*

"No."

Don't you feel that has something to do with your childhood? Is that why you don't think you need anyone?

"No. I am just that way."

So, if you're married, you don't feel like you have to tell your wife that you're going out of town?

"Yes, but if she doesn't want to come, I am gone."

I believe he meant exactly what he said.

As we were rapping up the interview, I leaned over and said, "Man, I hope that you find the love of your life." I began to pray and ask God to help him to experience the blessedness of real love, and really know that someone is going to be in his corner. But most of all, I wanted to convey to him that he must really learn to forgive others. Because forgiveness frees you to really live. I enjoyed this interview because he didn't pull any punches; he was rare and real.

Step-daughter A

I am Step daughter A, and it was crazy for me to even be going through this. When my dad and stepmom got married, I loved my stepmom, Claudia, but I wanted my mom and dad to still be married. Don't all kids? I am fifteen now, and it's a lot easier to share my heart.

1. *Were you angry when your mom and dad divorced?*

   - Yes, I thought it was my fault.

2. *How difficult was it to have to share the home you grew up in with other people? On top of that you now live in two different homes because the family had separated?*

   - I didn't feel it was fair for then to live in my house where I grew up and I have to move. That was my childhood home. It was hard and I was angry.

3. *How did you feel when you learned your dad was dating?*

   - It felt strange because I thought he would always be married to my mother. So, it was difficult to see him with another women laughing and enjoying himself.

-

4. *How did you feel when you were introduced to your dad's girlfriend for the first time?*

   - I was jealous and it made me mad. I was so confused.

5. *Since you were not used to having a lot of siblings, how difficult was it to adjust?*

   - Hmm… I don't do well with change, so I found it difficult because I had to learn to trust some new people. It was hard, but now that some time has passed, I love them all.

6. *How did you feel when you were first introduced to your dad's girlfriend's children?*

   - I liked them, but I didn't think they liked me.

7. *Did you find it difficult to have to share your dad with the other children?*

   -Yes. I felt like he was my dad and not theirs.

8. *Did you feel disloyal to your biological mom when you started to have feelings [of Love] for your stepmom?*
   - Sometimes.

9. *What's your take on being part of a blended family with a lot of children?*

   - It was crazy, for a while. Now, it's just lots love.

My Journey Through Divorce, Marriage and Blended Family

Ben*

Ben is the oldest biological son of his clan. He was always a daddy's boy. He missed his dad being in the home the most of his siblings.

1. *When did you realize your parent's weren't going to stay together?*

   - I realized that my parents were not getting back together after we moved in with our grandmother.

2. *How old were you?*

   - Six years old.

3. *Please give me your true feeling on divorce?*

   - Honestly, divorce is somewhat a good thing, but at times, it`s bad. I have mixed feelings because everybody was hurting and there was nothing we could do about it.

4. *Do you think you will ever get married?*
   - Yes, definitely.

5. *Did your parents handle you and your siblings in a caring way, during the period of pain, when your family was breaking up?*

   - Yes, they were always loving toward me, my brother and my sisters. I don`t know how they acted towards each other when we were not around.

6. *How is your relationship with your father since the divorce?*
   - I have a great relationship with my daddy.

7. *How is your relationship with your mom since the divorce?*
   - I have a good relationship with my mother; she has been my rock.

8. *Do you have an issue with trusting women because you had a broken home?*
   - I have my times that I don't trust women. But I am working on me.

9. *Is it hard for you to connect with the opposite sex because of what happen during your childhood?*
   - No not really, because I don't want my past to ruin my future.

My Journey Through Divorce, Marriage and Blended Family

Gordon*

Gordon is the youngest biological son of his clan, and was the least vocal of the six. He never said much. His mother had to keep a close eye on him emotionally because he didn't talk much. He always stayed under the wire, never causing a stir.

1. *Were you angry when you were told that your parents were divorcing?*

- Yes.

2. *Was the move from Atlanta to Alabama difficult?*

- Yes, because I loved living in Georgia.

3. *How did it make you feel to know your mom was dating?*

- It was weird to me to know my mom would be with another man other than my dad.

4. *Since you were already from a big family how was it to have more siblings?*

- Better because you know more people, but worst because you have more names and birthdays to remember.

5. *How did you feel when you met your mom's boyfriend's children?*

- It was a little weird because I didn't know them.

6. *Did you find it difficult to like or love your stepdad?*

- No, because Pop was a nice guy.

7. *Did you feel disloyal to your dad when you started having feelings (of love) for your stepfather?*

- No. I just had to figure out that he loved me and my dad did too. I didn't have to choose. All my parents loved me.

8. *Did you have a difficult time sharing your mom with other children?*

- Yes, I saw her as my mom, not theirs, but it changed along the way.

9. *Do you feel like this blended family thing worked for you?*

- Yes, I do. We fuss, but we are family, and we stick together.

Step-daughter B

This is step-daughter number four. She was the youngest daughter of her father's biological children. Described as "easy to love", she was a daddy's girl. She just wanted someone to love her, she gave her love freely.

1. *Where you angry when you first realized your parents were getting a divorce?*

   - Kind of, but I got over it.

2. *How difficult was it for you to move from your childhood home?*

   - I didn't move that was my home to. I lived with my mom, but I always spent a lot of time with my dad.

3. *How did you feel when your dad told you he was dating?*

   - I didn't have any negative feeling.

4. *How do you feel when you first meet your dad girlfriend?*

   - It was ok.

5. *Since you weren't from a really big family how was it to have so many sibling?*

- I was better and most of the time we were having fun.

6. *Did you find it difficult to love your step-mother?*

    - No, because she was very nice.

7. *Was it difficult for you to share your dad with your step-brothers and sister?*

    - Yes, because wasn't all about me anymore and now his attention was divided.

8. *Did you feel disloyal to your biological mother when you develop feeling for your step-mother?*

    - Yes because it felt strange.

9. *How do you feel about being in a blended family now that several years have passed?*

    - It's good most of the time.

A Teen's Story

I interviewed a teenager who has been going through a tough time as his parents are divorcing, so I promised not to release his name. I do want to express to this young person that things will get better if you want it to.

1. *When did you know your parents were going to divorce?*

   - When, every single night. I could hear the heated arguments and my dad was sleeping on the couch. And there were nights he didn't come home for days.

2. *How old were you at that time?*

   - I was fourteen years old.

3. *Please give your honest feelings on divorce.*

   - I am really against divorce, but in some situations, it is necessary. I believe once you say "I do," you should make sure, no matter what you go through, you should make sure your marriage works. When adults go through abuse or a cheating spouse, it will eventual go towards divorce.

4. *By your parents divorcing, does that change your outlook on relationships?*

   - Yes, by my parents divorcing, it made me have really bad trust issues. I am really picky about who I will talk to because I didn't want to partner with someone who don't love God. My father goes to church, but I don't believe he loves God. If he did, I don't believe he would be the man he has become today. Because of this, I don't handle arguments well. I just shut down. I really want that to change.

5. *Will you ever get married?*

   - Yes, of course.

6. *Did your mom and dad handle you in a caring way during that period of time?*

   - I am an only child from my mom and dad, but my dad has three other children. I have never lived with them. My mom always checked on me to make sure I was ok. She would always spend a lot of time with me, like going to movies, skating, bowling and shopping, and doing things I loved. She wanted me to know that both of us would be ok. My father didn't ask me about my feelings; he only cared about himself.

7. *How is your relationship with your dad?*

- My relationship with my dad is nonexistent. He has never really supported me. I have played basketball for nine years and he has only attended four games. He always has a way of getting me excited, and then he would tell a lie and just crush my hopes and dream. He would always tell me he was going to be there. I would keep asking my mom, "Where is my daddy?" I would be looking for his face in the crowd. He would always make up a lie and then try to spoil me with material things. Little did he know, the material things didn't heal my heart. And, the thing I wanted most was to have a relationship with him. I just wanted to be loved by him.

8. *How is your relationship with your mother?*

- The relationship with my mother is great. She has always made sure I was taken care of. I know I can go to my mom about anything. She is my role model and she has always tried to keep that gorgeous smile on her face, no matter what. My mom tried to make the relationship work because she wanted me to have both my parents in the same house. Because of the things my mom has had to go through, it has caused her to be a stronger woman, and it has caused me to be strong as well. I sometimes feel like a mirror image of her because, when she hurts, I hurt;

when she cries, I cry. We have an incredible bond.

9. *Is it hard for you to trust men?*

- Yes. There are times that I feel like the man I am with will do to me what my dad has done to my mom. I pray that when I marry, my husband won't do to me what my dad has done to my mom. I really don't want go through any of that; I just want to be happy.

10. *Is it hard for you to connect with young men because of what has happened to you as a child?*

- At first, but now I have realized that I am my own person. I can't keep letting things that have happened between my parents hold me back. I don't want my past to run off the man I love.

Opal's* Story

Opal is the third child in line of the biological children in her clan, and was very affected by her parents' toxic relationship. She had security issues (she always double checked the front door and windows after her parents had completed the task right in front of her). She also had trust issues because of her parents' broken relationship.

1. *Were you angry when you were first told that your parents were getting a divorce?*

   - No I wasn't angry. I was happy because all the fussing and fighting would be over.

2. *How hard was it to move in to another home?*
   - That was fine. But when we had to move to Alabama that was difficult because all my friends and family were in Atlanta.

3. *How did you feel when your mom started dating?*

   - It was a little weird at first, but I got used to it.

4. *How did you feel when you first met your mom's boyfriend?*

   - I liked him, and he seemed like a nice man.

5. *Since you were already from a big family, how did it feel to have more siblings?*

   - It wasn't bad, but I had to get used to more people in the house. But something about my mother, she was always helping someone, so people were always around.

   How did you feel when you first got a chance to meet your mom's boyfriend's children?

   - It was exciting for me to meet them those were my future sisters.

6. *Did you find it difficult to love your stepfather?*

   - I liked him, but I had to get used to him being around all the time. My dad worked all the time and mom was home with us.

7. *Was it difficult to have to learn to share your mom with the other children?*

   - No, it wasn't hard because we were used to having a lot of children around. Mom always had our friends and family at the house.

8. *Did you feel disloyal to you biological father for loving your stepfather?*

- No.

9. *Do you feel like the blended family you are a part of is working for you?*

   - Yes, it is working well!!!

Justine's* Story

Justine gave me such a good feeling during our interview. She is such a positive young person. Justine is sixteen years old and has such a great outlook on life. She inspired me to be a better person and to look at life through youthful eyes.

1. *How difficult was it to move from Florida to Georgia?*

- The move was very difficult because I loved living in my hometown. I still don't really like living in Georgia, but I love being with my family.

2. *How did you feel when you first heard your mom was dating?*

- It was ok with me.

3. *When you first meet the man your mom was dating, how did you feel?*

- Shy, because he was super tall.

4. *How did you feel when you met the other children of your stepdad?*

- My stepfather didn't have any children when they started dating. But, since we have become a family, my parents have had two little boys, who are my brothers.

5. *Did you find it difficult to love your stepfather and be loyal to your biological father?*

- Yes, sometimes. I just wanted everybody to be happy, and it all worked out for my family.

Fanny's* Story

Fanny is the youngest biological child of her clan. She was just figuring out who she was and how to feel about being the baby of family when her parents divorced. However, she knew how to express herself.

1. *How did you feel about your mom and dad breaking up?*

   - I am not sure. But I do remember all the fussing and fighting at the end of their marriage.

   2. *How did it affect you when your parents divorced?*

   -It hurt me, badly.

   3. *Do you feel that your parents handled you and your siblings in a caring way during the separation?*

   -My parents never talked badly about each other in my presence. I think they did the best they could. But that didn't make it any easier.

4. *Did you find it difficult not to live with both parents?*

   -Living in separate homes was difficult, until I realized that both of my parents loved me.

5. *Did you find it difficult to love both dads at same time?*

   -It wasn't hard to love both dads.

6. *How did you feel knowing mom was going to get married?*

   -Hurt and unsure of the new marriage. But I saw how happy mom was, so I was happy.

7. *Was it difficult to share your mom with your new siblings?*

   -Yes, the adjustment had to be made because mom belonged to all of us.

8. *How did you feel when you first met your mom's boyfriend's children?*

-It was ok because we started as friends and we grew on each other.

9. *How do you feel about your stepfather?*

-I had to learn that my stepdad was not just my friend, but my parent. I had to learn to listen and be respectful. My stepdad adds life to the family.

10. *How is your relationship with your mom since the divorce?*

-My mom is my rock. We don't always agree, but one thing I know, she loves me.

11. *How is your relationship with your biological dad since the divorce?*

   -What can I say? That's my daddy.

Fanny's advice: Being in a blended family is hard and difficult, but once you learn how to share, it makes life a lot easier.

CHAPTER 5
Heart of A Step-Parent

<u>Part A: Heart of A Dad and Divorced Man</u>

This is the story of a husband and his truth. It was hard to get him to do this interview because he didn't want his truth to offend his former wife or his daughters.

Life went from husband and wife to roommates. Our life was mom and dad to arguing and fussing. I was determined not to live that way anymore. We were in a constant battle in front of the children. It wasn't any way to live. We were tearing the children apart and I needed to make a decision. So I did.

I was married to a woman who didn't want to be a part of the biggest thing in my life. Other than my children, the ministry that God had put in me was my reason for being. My wife loved that I was a family man, and she had security, but she didn't want me. I needed someone who loved me for my heart, mind, body and soul. After my family, ministry was the biggest thing in my life and she didn't want any part of it. It was lonely, existing day, after day, living with someone who didn't like me. I needed someone in my life who wanted me, body, mind and soul.

She made her choice and I made mine. I'm not saying it was easy for either of us. The most important thing we needed to worry about were our girls.

Before anyone moved out of the family house, she moved into the extra room down the hallway. It seemed ok with her to live that way, but it wasn't ok with me. I didn't really ask her how she felt. We weren't speaking to each other, unless it was about the children. There wasn't much conversation about the move. One day, I came home and they were gone.

I continued on my journey, from this point, alone. She had the girls during the week, and I had them on the weekends. She stopped coming to church. So when the girls were with me, my pastor's wife and a good friend of mine would help me with the girls, if I needed it. I remember so many weekends when the girls and I would go to church, and they would sit alone on the pew. Some of the saints would watch them so I could preach.

We have to balance our lives and wear different hats: dad, husband, preacher and man. It wasn't easy, but I made it work. When you love your children, you will do whatever it takes to make the family work. The most important thing at that point was seeing my babies. There were many times during that process that my girls felt like they had to choose who to love, and that hurt me to see them hurt. It was difficult for them to learn to love both of us and that they didn't have to choose. We are both their parents, and just because we are not married anymore didn't mean that we didn't love them. Kids have a funny way of always making everything their fault. My daughter, Tiana, always wanted us to be together as a married couple and the divorce was really hard on her.

DON'T ALL CHILDREN WANT THEIR PARENTS TO BE MARRIED?

During the interview, my husband was sitting in his recliner, and I watched my husband's mind float way. I asked him what he was thinking about. He replied, "When I was married to my children's mother, what lesson were we teaching them as parents and what lesson will they carry into their relationships when they become adults?"

There are a great many things I am not able to speak about right now because I don't want to hurt my girls. But I will say one thing. God gave me the strength to make it through this without losing my mind. I would have loved to break the generational curse of divorce in my family. Since I wasn't able to do it, maybe my girls will.

Part B: Heart of A Stepmother

During my research for this book, I came across a stepmom who didn't want her name to be revealed, but she wanted her story to be heard. So we will call her Lady K. J. I really appreciate her allowing me to share her story with the world. As she began to tell her story, she immediately started crying.

Lady K.J. has been married for 20 years, and they had two children. She began her story by saying that her marriage had an expiration date. It was very hard for me to understand that statement, so she explained to me what she meant. She dated her husband for about two years before they were married, and all was well. She admitted to me during our conversation that they were sexually active before marriage. This information seemed to be very painful to share with me. During the 21st century that we live in, it is very normal for people to commit fornication. But during the time period that she grew up in, it was taboo. Prior to the marriage, they had great sex. The wedding date came, and it died. Her husband was very loving and caring; but after the nuptials, the intimacy disappeared. During the course of their marriage, they would only have sex once or twice a month. It was killing her inside to know that her husband, who she loved and shared a life with, didn't feel the same way about her.

My Journey Through Divorce, Marriage and Blended Family

How did you deal with the rejection from your husband and being around him every day?

We have two children and they deserve to have a two-parent home. One day, I finally couldn't take the rejection anymore. So, we separated. During our separation, I engaged in an extra martial affair with another man. He was a wonderful gentleman who loved me and physically wanted to be with me. He even wanted to marry me. When my kids were with their father, I had time to spend with this man and he allowed me to be who I wanted to be, in and out of the bed. One weekend, my boys returned home from a weekend with their father, and they were emotionally in disarray. The boys and I sat down and had a very frank conversation about why I couldn't be with their dad. My boys were very angry and disappointed in both of us. I allowed my children to vent and tell me how they really felt about the separation. It was a very difficult conversation. But because I loved them, I had to listen, not just hear. I really began to feel guilty about the choices I made for them, and not even considering how this would affect their lives as well. I realized that parents make decisions that the children have to just live with.

I reluctantly had to make a big decision in my relationship with my gentleman friend. I needed to get clear with God and to ask God for His forgiveness. I needed to put aside what I wanted and needed, and do what was best for my boys. The most important thing that I needed to remember was that my soul was in jeopardy of being lost.

If I didn't make the right decision, I could spend eternity in hell. That night after my boys went to bed, I called my friend and told him we could not see each other anymore. I could hear the hurt in his voice and it almost killed me to walk away from him. At that point, I knew I loved him, but I loved God more. That didn't make it hurt any less. I needed time to figure out what my next move should be. I made my choice and I intended to keep my vow to God. I know it sounds crazy. I had already broken my marriage vows. I thank God that He is a forgiving and kind. It took me some time to let my heart catch up with my decision. I began to seek God for answers on giving my marriage another chance.

Lady K.J knew God wasn't pleased with the broken home they had both created. The question she asked me during the interview was, "How I can glorify God if I am so unhappy?" My reply was not to ask me. Ask God what He desired, and then ask Him to help you to accept His will. I don't really know if I could give her any other answer because I was in an unhappy marriage for many years. Who was I to give any advice? After a few moments of silence, she began to tell what happened.

"God spoke to me a few weeks later, and I called my husband and explained to him what was going on with me. I told my husband that we needed to talk. He agreed to meet with me while the kids were in school so we could talk freely.

My Journey Through Divorce, Marriage and Blended Family

"We met at a local restaurant outside of Atlanta. When he came over to me, I was very anxious because we hadn't spoken to each in a long time (unless it was about the children). I was very uncomfortable, and he seemed not to really even want to be there.

"I needed to come clean and let him know what had been going on with me. During the conversation, he began to tell me that he had been dating, but it wasn't serious yet. While we were talking, we made a decision that we would start seeing each other.

"I was doing this, at first, for the kids. But when we started seeing each other, he really seemed to have changed. The best thing about this new relationship with my husband was that he was very forgiving of my mistakes, and that I was going to have to follow suit, and give him another chance too. We dated for a few months before we were involved in any physical relationship. I needed to know that he saw me for who I was and not the old wife he had. During the trial of dating my husband, it made me feel like a teenager again. When we had our first night together, he made me feel like I was the only woman in the world. After that night, he asked me if would I come home and try again. While he was talking to me, I just kept wondering if things would be different this time. My husband promised me things would be better.

"We told the boys together, and they were so happy we couldn't pack fast enough."

Did you really want to move back in so quickly?

"No, but my boys were so happy to see us together. How could I say no?

"Some time had passed, and things began to go back to the way they were before the separation. He wasn't paying any attention to me, and the love making was little to none at all. The same issue started coming up and I didn't know what to say or do about this dilemma. But I knew God hadn't forgotten about me. This broken vessel asked God for strength to endure this life. It was so hard to lay next to a man who, whenever I touched him, acted like his skin was crawling.

"We have one son in college, the other will graduate in a few months, and one son will be going to college in few years. The expiration date of this marriage is the day that our youngest son goes to college."

My Journey Through Divorce, Marriage and Blended Family

<u>Lewis* and Marcia's* Story</u>

Lewis and his wife, Marcia, sat down with me one Sabbath (Saturday) afternoon, and allowed me to pick his brain about how he and his wife got together.

Lewis was very familiar with the triangle of a blended family. I never knew until this interview that his older brother wasn't his dad's biological child. (His mother was pregnant when his dad met her.) When I am around his family I could never tell. I have been around his family for years and they blended very well. I really admired his dad for that type of love and teaching to his children.

Lewis was five years old before he even realized that his older brother was not his dad's biological son. He found out listening to a conversation between his other siblings. He didn't really believe it at first because you wouldn't know the difference between the biological and the spiritual children – that's the kind of dad John Smith is.

Lewis said the conversation went on and nothing ever changed in the family because that was their brother. That's what makes that marriage special to me.

Lewis and Marcia met in the year of 2002 and they were married by 2005. They were introduced by a family member at a wedding. Marcia had one daughter and her name was Willa*.

How long did you guys date before you met her daughter Willa, face-to-face?

- We dated about two months before I met Willa. Marcia and Willa were living in Florida, at the time. But I was able to talk with her on the phone. I think I talked more to Willa then Marcia. Before meeting her, I wanted to make sure the relationship was progressing towards a serious relationship. I was very concerned about not hurting Willa or Marcia.

Were you dating with the intention of searching for a girlfriend or a wife?

- I was looking for my soul mate and I found her.

Was there ever a time you thought Willa was confused about when to call you dad?

- Yes. Once we were visiting in Florida, at a family gathering. Her biological father and I were in the same room, and she said, "Dad". Both of us turned around. After that, she started calling me Daddy Lew. That never changed how I felt about my daughter; I loved her just the same.

Has there ever been a time when you guys had a struggle as a couple because she wasn't your biological child?

- Never, because Marcia and I talked about how we would raise our children before we got married.

If you set the foundation and stay on course, you won't go wrong. My wife and I knew what we wanted of family life, and marriage from the beginning.

During this blending of the family, was there ever a time which Willa tried to challenge your authority as a parent?

- I can only remember one incident. My mother-in-law was in town, visiting. She is Willa's best buddy. One evening, I had cooked and prepared dinner for the family. Willa came downstairs to eat dinner and she made a comment, "I would rather starve than to eat that." I told her, "This is what we will do. How about you won't eat in this house at all?" So that went on for about two days. The only time that she ate was at school or if she wasn't home. My wife and I spoke with Willa and explained to her that God has provided for all of us and we must learn to be respectful to what He has given us. The crazy thing about it was it was just a regular meal that she would not eat.

During the interview, Willa came over. I asked her about the dinner incident. She said one thing that she had learned after she apologized was that daddy meant what he said, and mom stood by him. "I didn't have a chance."

Lewis has a wonderful relationship with Willa and you can't tell that he's her stepfather. I enjoyed the interview because it was raw and truthful. It was especially good because his wife and daughter were able to give me insight into what kind of father he is, especially what type of man he is. This was special for me to do this interview. I wish we all could have a happy ending.

CHAPTER 6

The Do's and Don'ts of

Blended Family

Do's

1. LOVE, LOVE, LOVE
2. Communication
3. Learn to communicate
4. Foster lots of family time
5. Always make special time for each individual child
6. Allow children to have a voice (teach them to do it respectfully)
7. LAUGH, LAUGH, LAUGH
8. PRAY, PRAY, PRAY
9. The most important **DO** is that God is the head of the family
10. Parents (biological and step-parent): it is a must that they work together
11. Husbands and wives need date night (make your marriage a priority)
12. Use all the tools available to you to help your blended family work such as pastors and other

church leaders, school counselors, and child psychologists

13. Learn to forgive **quickly**
14. **All fighting isn't bad**

Don'ts

1. Parents never put the children in the middle of an argument
2. Never use the children as weapon against the other parent
3. Step-parents: never make the step-child/children feel unloved or different than your biological child/children
4. Never buy items for biological children/child, but not for the stepchildren
5. Parents and children/child: never think you have all of the answers
6. Don't be afraid to ask for help
7. Parents: never take sides when the children are in a disagreement
8. Parents: don't argue in front of the children
9. Last, but not least: never leave God out of your marriage and family

My Journey Through Divorce, Marriage and Blended Family

ABOUT THE AUTHOR

Claudette T. Mullgrav Hutchinson is a life experience expert. Having been married twice, she has born six children, mothered four more, and mentored and loved 17 others. A foster system, and sexual and mental abuse survivor, Claudette knows the importance of strong family bonds and unconditional love, so she has made both the basis of her parenting. It is no surprise that Claudette's calling in life is to minister hurt and untethered young people. She has taken her calling seriously, and is an ordained minister and certified life coach.

Claudette is the first to tell you that accepting one's calling doesn't insulate you from pain or suffering. Losing a child was one of the most devastating times of her life. But she knows that through Christ's love, all hurts may be healed. Claudette is most joyful about her life as it is now because she didn't just survive all she has endured, she is healthy and whole.

www.ingramcontent.com/pod-product-compliance
Lightning Source LLC
LaVergne TN
LVHW021613080426
835510LV00019B/2550